WE COME FROM

Germany

MIKE HIRST

RSVP
RAINTREE
STECK-VAUGHN
PUBLISHERS
A Steck-Vaughn Company

Austin, Texas

WE COME FROM

Brazil • China • France
Germany • India • Jamaica • Japan
Kenya • Nigeria • South Africa

The people you are about to meet live in a village in Germany called Bergshausen. Like any other country, Germany has many different lifestyles. People live in towns and cities as well as in the country.

Cover: Moritz, Lisa, and some friends get ready for a game of croquet.
Title page: From top to bottom: An old windmill in Kassel; the stock exchange in Frankfurt; a busy café in Bremen; a canalside in Hamburg; and a shopping street in Bremen
Contents page: These shoppers are taking a break beside a sculpture of pigs in Hamburg.
Index: The Parisius family has a picnic lunch near a local river.

Published by Raintree Steck-Vaughn Publishers, an imprint of Steck-Vaughn Company

Printed in Italy. Bound in the United States.
1 2 3 4 5 6 7 8 9 0 04 03 02 01 00

Library of Congress Cataloging-in-Publication Data
Hirst, Mike.
Germany / Mike Hirst.
    p.   cm.—(We come from)
    Includes bibliographical references and index.
    Summary: An introduction to the geography, climate, schools, sports, food, recreation, and culture of Germany.
    ISBN 0-8172-5218-5
    1. Germany—Juvenile literature.
    [1. Germany.]
    I. Title. II. Series.
DD17.H57 1999
943—dc21   98-31934

Picture Acknowledgments: All the photographs in this book were taken by Steve Benbow. The map artwork on page 4 is produced by Peter Bull.

Contents

Welcome to Germany

"My name is Moritz. I'm here with my family and my dog, Paula, in our backyard."—Moritz

Moritz Parisius is nine years old. He lives with his parents and his older sister, Lisa. They have a dog named Paula and a cat named Söcke (*Socks*). The family lives in a village called Bergshausen, in the middle of Germany. You can see where it is on the map on page 5.

▲ *From left to right: Moritz's dad, Moritz, Moritz's mom, Moritz's sister, Lisa.*

▶ *Germany's place in the world*

▼ *Germany is a large country in the middle of Europe.*

GERMANY

Capital city:	Berlin
Land area:	137,848 sq. mi. (357,000 sq. km)
Population:	82 million people
Main language:	German
Main religions:	Roman Catholic (in the south) and Protestant (in the north)

The Land and Weather

Germany is in the middle of Europe. The north of Germany is bordered by the sea, and the land is flat. There are lots of hills in the center of Germany, and in the south there are high mountains.

Around Bergshausen, the land is hilly. There are fields and woods outside the village.

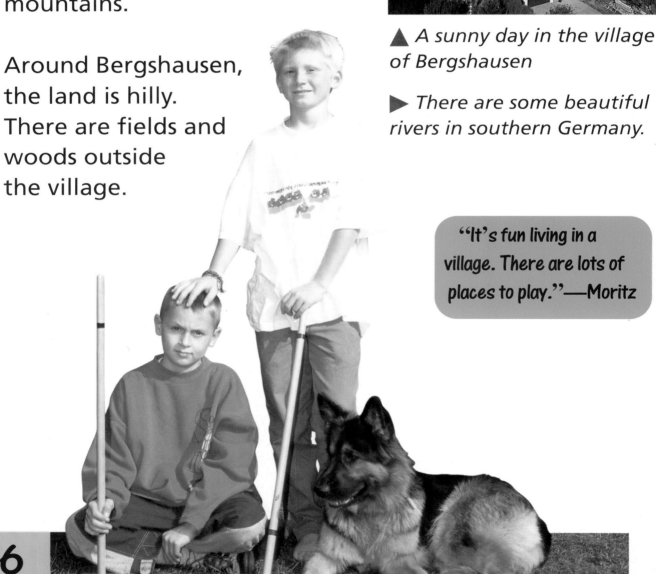

▲ *A sunny day in the village of Bergshausen*

▶ *There are some beautiful rivers in southern Germany.*

"It's fun living in a village. There are lots of places to play."—Moritz

7

◄During the summer, many Germans go to the beaches in the north.

The weather in Germany changes from one time of the year to another. Summer is usually warm and sunny. Winter is much colder. There is ice and snow, especially in the high mountains in the south of Germany.

▼ Moritz and Lisa go for a bicycle ride in the autumn rain.

Just a short distance away from Bergshausen lies the city of Kassel. Most Germans live in large cities or towns, such as Kassel.

▲ *There are many stores and offices in Kassel's busy center.*

At Home

In Germany many people rent their homes. In towns and cities most people live in apartments instead of houses. The people who live in apartments don't have yards, but some have balconies.

▲ *Each apartment has a doorbell and mailbox by the main entrance. Each family's name is next to its bell.*

▶ *In busy cities apartments jostle for space with tall office buildings.*

"We come to our local park when we want to play outside."
—Sonja (right)

11

▶ *These old houses in Bergshausen have wooden frames.*

▼ *Moritz and Lisa enjoy watching television in their living room.*

The Parisius family lives in a modern house. Mr. and Mrs. Parisius do not want their home to harm the environment. They try not to use too much gas and electricity.

Like many other German families, the Parisius family can afford expensive goods, such as a car, a television set, and a computer.

▼ *Sometimes Moritz finds some interesting creatures, like this hedgehog, in the garden.*

German Food

Germans enjoy their food, and they are proud of their country's special dishes.

German people buy lots of their food in supermarkets, but there are still many small stores, too. Most neighborhoods have their own baker and butcher.

▲ *Favorite evening snacks are sausages, dark pumpernickel bread, and pickled fish.*

▶ *Fresh fruit and vegetables are sold at colorful outdoor markets.*

◀ *Customers choose their own vegetables at the supermarket.*

▲ The Parisius family sits down to a traditional breakfast.

The Parisius family often has a large breakfast, with boiled eggs, bread, and cheese. There is sometimes ham or meat paste, too.

Many Germans like to have a cooked meal at lunchtime. In towns and cities, hungry office workers crowd into cafés or busy restaurants.

▶ On warm days, you can have lunch at an outdoor café.

"People come to my stand for a snack of sausage and bread."
— Mr. Graf, food stand owner

At Work

Industries making goods such as cars, electrical goods, and machinery provide many jobs in Germany.

▼ *At the stock exchange in Frankfurt, people invest money in German industries.*

In Bergshausen, some people work on the farms in the village. Many others work at a large car factory nearby.

Moritz's mother works as a kind of doctor called a psychiatrist. On some days she works in an office that is part of the Parisius home.

◀ *Mr. Schmidt is a pig farmer in Bergshausen.*

19

At School

German children begin school by going part-time to a nursery called a *kindergarten*. Elementary school starts when they are six years old.

▶ *Children crowd onto a bus to be taken to school.*

▼ *These children are hard at work, building a model rocket.*

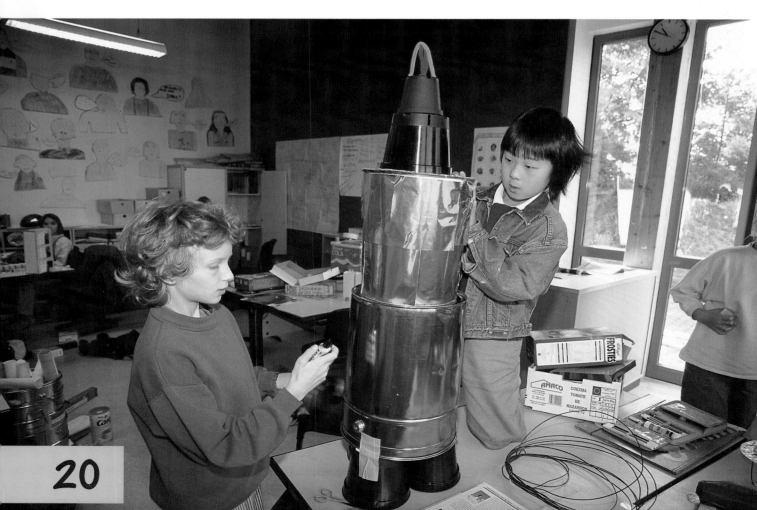

The school day begins at eight o'clock in the morning. There are classes all morning, with two short breaks. When classes finish at one o'clock, the children go home in time for lunch.

▲ *Children work in pairs on the school computers.*

21

◄ There are about 25 boys and girls in Moritz's class.

Moritz has just started at a new school. It is in the nearby town of Kassel. He travels there every day by bus.

Moritz's school is in a brand-new building. There is plenty of modern equipment, and each class has its own computers.

▼ Every afternoon, Moritz has to do some homework.

"I like art and English, but my favorite subject is soccer!"— Moritz

23

Free Time

Sports are very popular in Germany, especially soccer and swimming.

Bergshausen has its own youth club, run by the local church. Children go there to play games such as table tennis.

▲ *Lisa is learning to play the mandolin in her spare time.*

"If the weather's good, we all go out fishing together."—Moritz

▶ *This girl is learning how to unicycle at a youth club.*

24

25

Looking Ahead

Germany is a modern, wealthy country. Its factories make goods such as cars, mobile phones, and hi-fi equipment. These things are sold all over the world.

Many Germans are worried about the harm that cars and industry can do to the environment. They want to stop pollution in towns and cities.

"When I grow up, I want to play soccer for Germany!"—Moritz

▶ New buildings shoot up in Berlin, Germany's capital.

Holiday Cookies

Moritz and his family like to eat holiday cookies during the Christmas season. They are very easy to make.

You will need:

7 Tablespoons (100 g) butter
6 Tablespoons (75 g) sugar
1 egg
$1\frac{1}{3}$ cups (200 g) flour
half teaspoon mixed spice
half teaspoon ground cinnamon
1–2 tablespoons of milk

- First, cream the butter and sugar together in a mixing bowl.

▲ *Moritz starts to make the dough.*

- Then, separate the egg yolk and beat it into the mixture. Sift in the flour and spices and mix well. Add the milk and knead the mixture into a soft dough.

- Roll out the mixture on a floured board, until it is about $\frac{1}{4}$ in. (5 mm) thick. Cut out star or moon shapes. Brush the top of each shape with the egg white.

- Ask an adult to bake the cookies for 10 to 12 minutes at 375° F.

▲ *Moritz's mother and sister use oven mitts to take the cookies out of the hot oven.*

Germany Fact File

Money Facts

◄ German money is the mark, which is divided into 100 pfennigs. $1 is worth about 1.65 marks. Karl Friedrich Gauss, the famous mathematician, can be seen on the 10 mark note.

Famous People
Famous German people include Johann Gutenberg, who invented the printing press during the fifteenth century, and the Brothers Grimm, who wrote *Grimm's Fairy Tales*. Tennis champions Boris Becker and Steffi Graf are both from Germany.

River Facts
Germany has several major rivers, such as the Rhine, the Elbe, and the Danube.

The German Flag
▼ The red, black, and gold represent a long struggle for a united Germany.

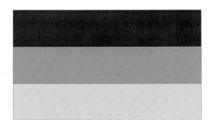

Mountain Facts
The highest mountain is the Zugspitze, in the Alps. It is 9,721 ft. (2,963 m) high.

The Berlin Wall
After World War II, Germany was divided into East Germany and West Germany. In 1961, East Germany's government built a wall through Berlin to stop its people from going to West Germany. In 1990 East Germany and West Germany became one country again and the Berlin Wall was torn down. ▼

Car Industry
Germany is famous for producing high-quality cars, which are sold all over the world.

Delicatessen
Germans make different types of delicious sausages, from *bratwurst* to *salami*. ▼

Glossary

Balconies Special areas outside apartment windows where people can sit, hang laundry, or grow plants.

Environment The surrounding area. It includes the land, air, and water around where you live.

Invest To put money into businesses to make more money.

Mandolin An old-fashioned stringed instrument.

Pollution Anything that can harm the natural environment.

Psychiatrist A doctor who treats illnesses of the mind.

Rent To pay money to the owner of a house in order to live there.

Unicycle A cycle with only one wheel. Unicycles are very difficult to balance.

Further Information

Fiction:

Any of the *Grimm's Fairy Tales*.

Non-fiction:

Arnow, Helen. *Postcards from Germany* (Postcards). Austin, TX: Raintree Steck-Vaughn, 1997.

Cumming, David. *Germany* (Modern Industrial World). Austin, TX: Raintree Steck-Vaughn, 1994.

Morris, Ting. *Germany* (Country Topics for Craft Projects). Danbury, CT: Franklin Watts, 1994.

Peters, Sonja. *A Family from Germany* (Families Around the World). Austin, TX: Raintree Steck-Vaughn, 1998.

Useful Addresses:

German Embassy
4645 Reservoir Rd., NW
Washington, DC 20007
(202) 298-4000

German National Tourist Office
122 E. 42nd Street
New York, NY 10019
(212) 661-7200

Index

All the numbers in **bold** refer to photographs.